STUDY GUIDE

Rethinking GOD with Tacos

Copyright © 2025 by Jason Clark

Published by UNORTHODOX Resources

All rights reserved. No portion of this book may be reproduced, stored in a retrieval system, or transmitted in any form or by any means—electronic, mechanical, photocopy, recording, scanning, or other—except for brief quotations in critical reviews or articles, without prior written permission of the author.

Unless otherwise noted, all Scripture quotations are taken from the Holy Bible, New International Version®, NIV®. Copyright © 1973, 1978, 1984, 2011 by Biblica, Inc.™ Used by permission of Zondervan. All rights reserved worldwide. www.zondervan.com. The "NIV" and "New International Version" are trademarks registered in the United States Patent and Trademark Office by Biblica, Inc.™ | Scripture quotations marked BSB are from The Holy Bible, Berean Study Bible, BSB, Copyright ©2016, 2020 by Bible Hub Used by Permission. All Rights Reserved Worldwide. | Scripture quotations marked KJV are taken from the King James Version of the Bible. Public domain. | Scripture quotations marked NKJV are taken from the New King James Version®. Copyright © 1982 by Thomas Nelson. Used by permission. All rights reserved.

For foreign and subsidiary rights, contact the author.

Cover design by: Todd Petelle
Cover photo by: Seth Snider

ISBN: 978-1-964794-01-3   1 2 3 4 5 6 7 8 9 10

Printed in the United States of America

STUDY GUIDE

Rethinking GOD with Tacos

Jason Clark

UNORTHODOX RESOURCES

CONTENTS

Chapter 1.	**WHAT IS THE GOSPEL?**	8
Chapter 2.	**THE CROSS**	14
Chapter 3.	**UNION**	20
Chapter 4.	**A CHRISTOLOGICAL HERMENEUTIC**	26
Chapter 5.	**RELATIONAL THEOLOGY**	32
Chapter 6.	**ON DECONSTRUCTION**	38
Chapter 7.	**TRINITARIAN FAITH**	44
Chapter 8.	**THE INCARNATION**	50
Chapter 9.	**IDENTITY**	56
Chapter 10.	**A PATH TO WHOLENESS**	62
Chapter 11.	**THE CHURCH**	68
Chapter 12.	**THE KINGDOM**	74
Chapter 13.	**GRACE**	80
Chapter 14.	**INCLUSION**	86
Chapter 15.	**RETHINKING UNIVERSALISM**	92
Chapter 16.	**RETHINKING HELL**	98
Chapter 17.	**JUSTICE**	104
Chapter 18.	**THE LONG ARC OF LOVE**	110

CHAPTER 1

WHAT IS THE GOSPEL?
Taco 'Bout the Good News

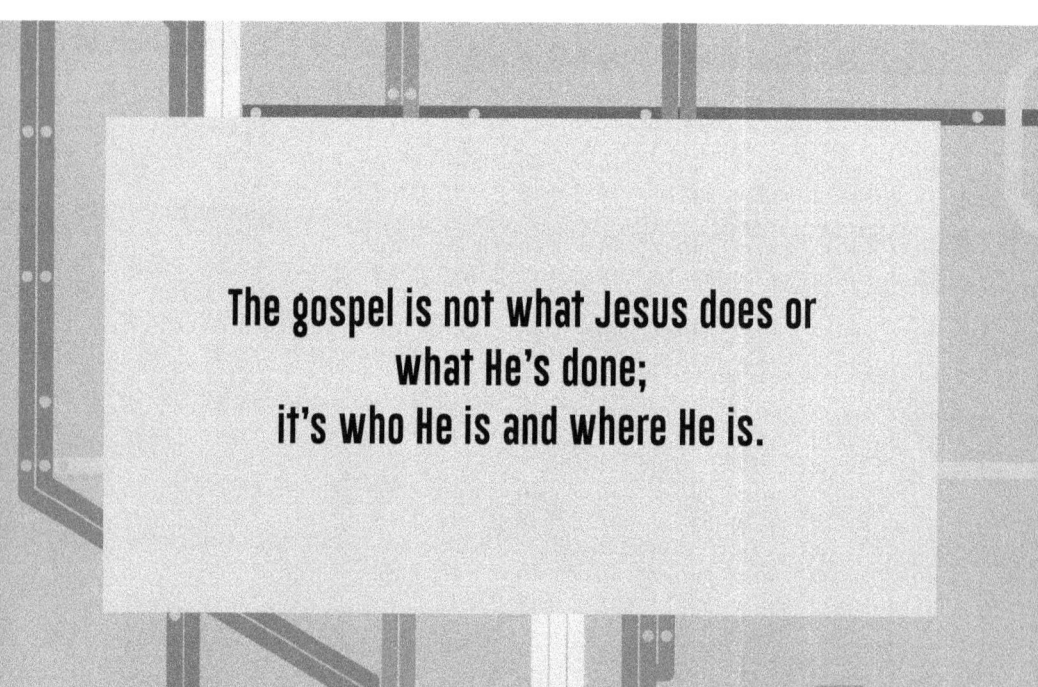

The gospel is not what Jesus does or what He's done;
it's who He is and where He is.

READING TIME

As you read Chapter 1: "What Is the Gospel?" in *Rethinking GOD with Tacos*, reflect on, and respond to the text by answering the following questions.

REFLECT AND TAKE ACTION:

Did a "religion of separation" define your early understanding of God and the Church? How has that framework affected your current relationship with Him?

_____
_____
_____
_____
_____
_____
_____
_____

When have you mistaken the pain of institutional dismissal for the character of God? How does the character of Jesus, not the institution, reshape your frame of reference for who God is?

_____
_____
_____
_____
_____
_____
_____
_____

> *"Every good and perfect gift is from above, coming down from the Father of the heavenly lights, who does not change like shifting shadows."*
>
> **—James 1:17 (NIV)**

Consider the scripture above and answer the following questions:

How does this scripture challenge the way you have always viewed the love of God? How does it contrast to the changing and often hurtful portrayals of Him you may have grown up with?

_____
_____
_____
_____
_____
_____
_____

How do you reconcile God as the provider of "every good and perfect gift" with a God who judges and excludes?

_____
_____
_____
_____
_____
_____
_____

Have you ever believed God had turned His back on you? What evidence in your life challenges that belief and points instead to His nearness?

_____
_____
_____
_____
_____
_____
_____
_____
_____
_____
_____

If Jesus is the full and final Word on who God is, what parts of your theology or assumptions about God need to be unlearned or reimagined?

___

In what ways have you unknowingly carried a gospel of fear and separation instead of the good news of union and friendship?

___

Where in your life do you sense God inviting you to exchange your narrow perspective for His eternal one? What holds you back from accepting it?

_____
_____
_____
_____
_____
_____
_____
_____

Which part of this chapter disrupted your assumptions or stirred something uncomfortable in you? Why?

_____
_____
_____
_____
_____
_____
_____
_____

CHAPTER 2

THE CROSS
Where Love Set the Table

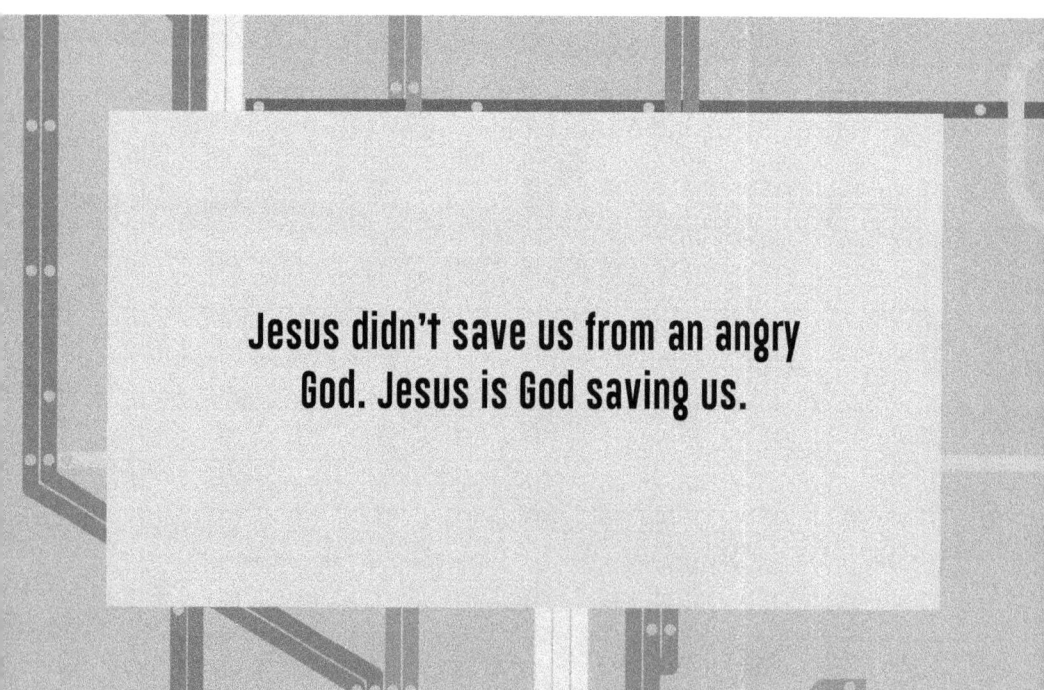

Jesus didn't save us from an angry God. Jesus is God saving us.

READING TIME

As you read Chapter 2: "The Cross" in *Rethinking GOD with Tacos*, reflect on, and respond to the text by answering the following questions.

REFLECT AND TAKE ACTION:

What early messages did you receive about the cross? Did they frame it as both an act of love and an expression of divine punishment? What image of God emerges as you view Him through that lens?

_____
_____
_____
_____
_____
_____
_____
_____

How does the idea that "Jesus is God saving us," not "Jesus is saving us from God," challenge your theology or upbringing?

_____
_____
_____
_____
_____
_____
_____
_____
_____

> *"My God, My God, why have You forsaken Me?... He has not despised nor abhorred the affliction of the afflicted; Nor has He hidden His face from Him; But when He cried to Him, He heard"*
>
> **—Psalm 22:1, 24 (NKJV)**

Consider the scripture above and answer the following questions:

How does the inclusion of both verses reshape the meaning of Jesus's cry on the cross?

_____
_____
_____
_____
_____
_____
_____
_____

What does it reveal about the heart of God that Jesus, while dying a brutal death, quoted a Psalm to affirm God's nearness?

_____
_____
_____
_____
_____
_____
_____
_____

When you view the cross through the lens of union instead of separation, how does it change the way you pray, worship, or relate to God?

_____

_____

_____

_____

_____

_____

_____

_____

_____

_____

What would shift in your life if you truly believed there is no distance between you and the Father—not even in your worst moments?

_____
_____
_____
_____
_____
_____
_____
_____

Can you think of an area in your life where you still approach God from a place of fear rather than trust? What does God want to show you about His heart in that specific area of your life?

_____
_____
_____
_____
_____
_____
_____
_____

In what ways have you feared God's judgment rather than trusted His healing love? Provide an example. How baked in is that belief, and how would you challenge it now?

_____
_____
_____
_____
_____
_____
_____
_____

In what ways has penal substitutionary atonement theology influenced how you see yourself in relation to God? What new understanding is emerging through this chapter?

_____
_____
_____
_____
_____
_____
_____
_____

CHAPTER 3

UNION
One Shell, a Lot of Love

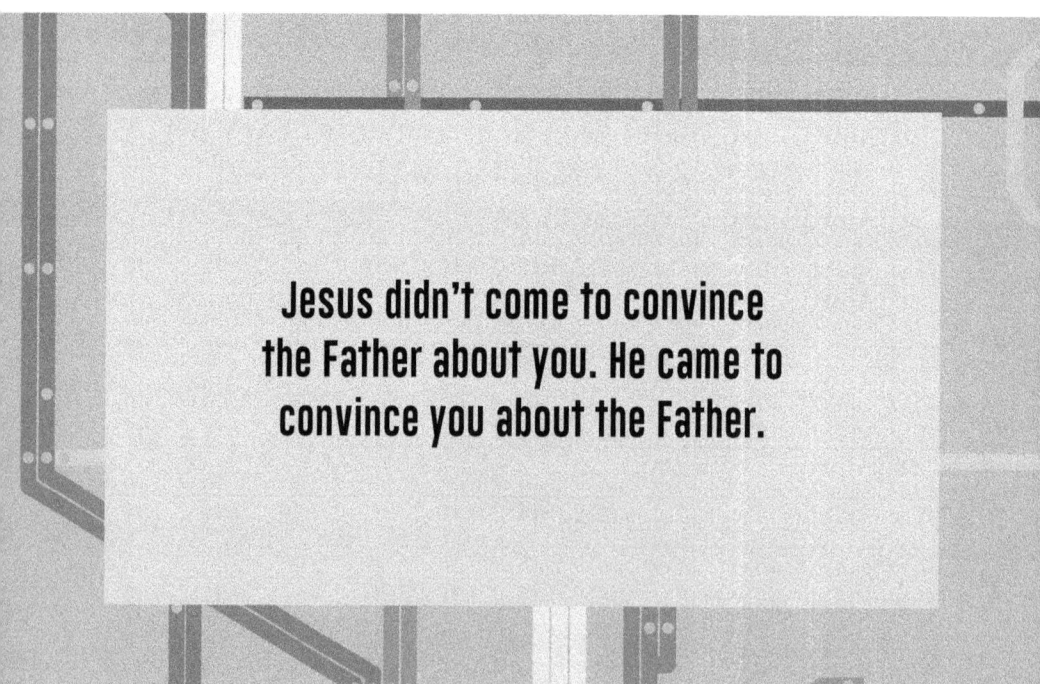

Jesus didn't come to convince the Father about you. He came to convince you about the Father.

READING TIME

As you read Chapter 3: "The Union" in *Rethinking GOD with Tacos*, reflect on, and respond to the text by answering the following questions.

REFLECT AND TAKE ACTION:

Have you ever believed you needed to work your way closer to God? Share a specific example. Did that approach bring lasting peace, or did it lead to more striving and exhaustion in your relationship with Him?

_____
_____
_____
_____
_____
_____
_____
_____

How have the lies of "distance and delay" shaped your spiritual walk? In what ways are you now learning to rest in what's already true?

_____
_____
_____
_____
_____
_____
_____
_____

> *"And God raised us up with Christ and seated us with Him in the heavenly realms in Christ Jesus."*
>
> —**Ephesians 2:6 (NIV)**

Consider the scripture above and answer the following questions:

If you are already seated with Christ, for what reason might you still feel like you're standing outside the room trying to earn a place at the table?

_____
_____
_____
_____
_____
_____
_____
_____

How does your daily life reflect (or deny) the truth that you share the same seated position as Christ?

_____
_____
_____
_____
_____
_____
_____
_____

Do you live and pray like someone who is seated with Jesus—or like someone still begging for access?

_____
_____
_____
_____
_____
_____
_____

Take a moment to pause and imagine the scene described in this chapter: a throne room where Jesus is seated on the throne. Picture the space. Picture Him. Then, place yourself somewhere in that room—anywhere. Answer the following questions:

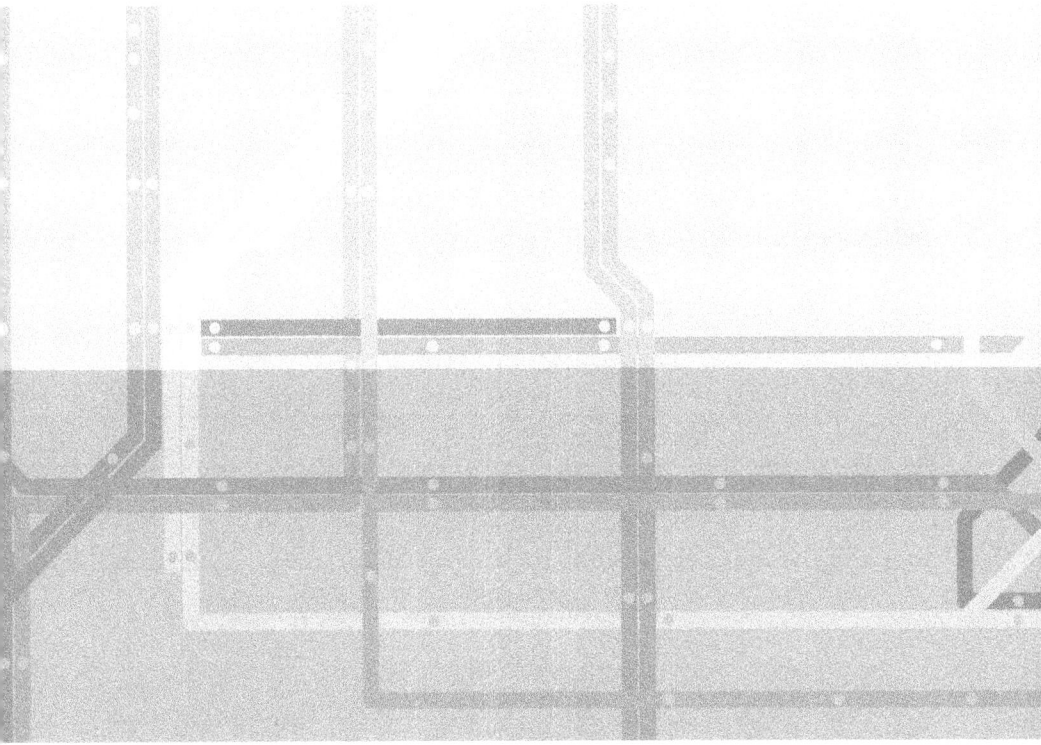

Where did you find yourself? At the edge of the room, near a door, at His feet, beside Him—or even seated with Him?

_____
_____
_____
_____
_____
_____
_____
_____
_____

What does your position in the room reveal about how you currently view Jesus? What does it reveal about how you believe Jesus views you?

_____
_____
_____
_____
_____
_____
_____
_____
_____

To what extent did your vision align with or conflict with the truth of Ephesians 2:6?

_____
_____
_____
_____
_____
_____
_____
_____
_____

Which part of this chapter disrupted your understanding of God or yourself—and what are you going to do with that disruption?

_____
_____
_____
_____
_____
_____
_____
_____
_____

CHAPTER 4

A CHRISTOLOGICAL HERMENEUTIC
Seeing Christ in Every Bite

The Bible minus love equals
false teaching.

READING TIME

As you read Chapter 4: "A Christological Hermeneutic" in *Rethinking GOD with Tacos*, reflect on, and respond to the text by answering the following questions.

REFLECT AND TAKE ACTION:

What do you think it means for Jesus to be "the whole story"? How do you reconcile that truth with passages in the Old Testament that seem to portray God as harsh, distant, or punitive?

_____
_____
_____
_____
_____
_____
_____
_____

To what extent have you given equal theological weight to Job, the Book of Leviticus, and Jesus? What has led you to do that—and what's changed?

_____
_____
_____
_____
_____
_____
_____
_____

> *"For I resolved to know nothing while I was with you except Jesus Christ and him crucified."*
>
> **—1 Corinthians 2:2 (NIV)**

Consider the scripture above and answer the following questions:

If Jesus—especially Jesus crucified—is the only thing Paul resolved to know and preach, what does that say about how we should interpret the rest of Scripture?

_____
_____
_____
_____
_____
_____
_____
_____

How do your current beliefs about God compare to the Jesus revealed on the cross? Do they align—or do they compete?

_____
_____
_____
_____
_____
_____
_____
_____

What would it look like to interpret difficult or violent scriptures through the lens of the crucified Christ?

_____
_____
_____
_____
_____
_____
_____
_____
_____
_____
_____

What specific passages or stories in the Bible have caused you to struggle with the character of God? Read that passage again, this time through the lens of Jesus—His life, love, and character—and describe what you see differently.

_____
_____
_____
_____
_____
_____
_____
_____

What does it mean to you that "the Bible isn't the Word of God—Jesus is"? How does that change your posture toward Scripture?

_____
_____
_____
_____
_____
_____
_____
_____

What fears come up when you consider letting go of a literal or "flat" reading of Scripture in favor of a love-based, Christological lens?

_____
_____
_____
_____
_____
_____
_____
_____

Now that you've read this chapter, what's one practical step you can take to begin (or continue) reading the Bible with Jesus as your only hermeneutic?

_____
_____
_____
_____
_____
_____
_____
_____

CHAPTER 5

RELATIONAL THEOLOGY
Tortillas Together

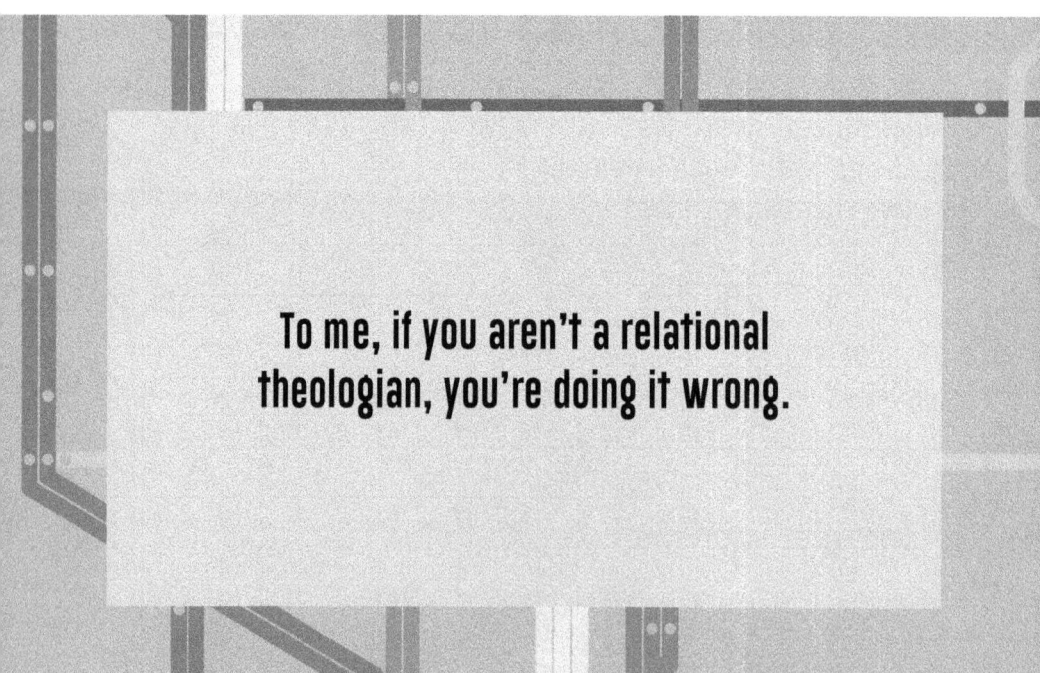

To me, if you aren't a relational theologian, you're doing it wrong.

READING TIME

As you read Chapter 5: "Relational Theology" in *Rethinking GOD with Tacos*, reflect on, and respond to the text by answering the following questions.

REFLECT AND TAKE ACTION:

How has your experience in church shaped your view of theology? Has it felt more like a sterile system or a living relationship?

_____
_____
_____
_____
_____
_____
_____
_____

What emotions surfaced as you read the idea that if you're not a relational theologian, you're doing it wrong? What does that challenge in you?

_____
_____
_____
_____
_____
_____
_____
_____

Have you ever felt disqualified from theological conversations because of your personality, wiring, or lack of formal training? How does this chapter invite you to reframe that?

Brad Jersak speaks about "consenting love"—a love that never forces. Can you identify areas where you've said "yes" to God? How has He responded to your consent?

How does the idea that "our actions affect God" shift your understanding of His nature and your own agency in relationship with Him?

Jonathan Foster describes God as one who waits for our "yes" and honors our voice in the story. Where in your life do you sense God is waiting for your permission to move?

_____
_____
_____

Ryan Pena shared, "There are pages in your heart I didn't author." What pages in your life might God be inviting you to rewrite with Him?

_____
_____
_____
_____

What lies about God's character or your identity has He been gently erasing over time? What truth is He replacing them with?

_____
_____
_____
_____
_____
_____
_____
_____

Relational theology often embraces paradox and mystery over certainty. Where in your walk with God have you been uncomfortable with mystery? How might the unknown aspects of God actually strengthen intimacy instead of weakening it?

_____
_____
_____
_____
_____
_____
_____
_____

Reflect on the statement: "Control is the antithesis of relational trust." In what areas are you still trying to give God control rather than embracing union and self-control?

_____
_____
_____
_____
_____
_____
_____
_____

After reading this chapter, what does it mean to you personally to be a relational theologian?

_____
_____
_____
_____
_____
_____
_____
_____

CHAPTER 6

ON DECONSTRUCTION
Taco Salad

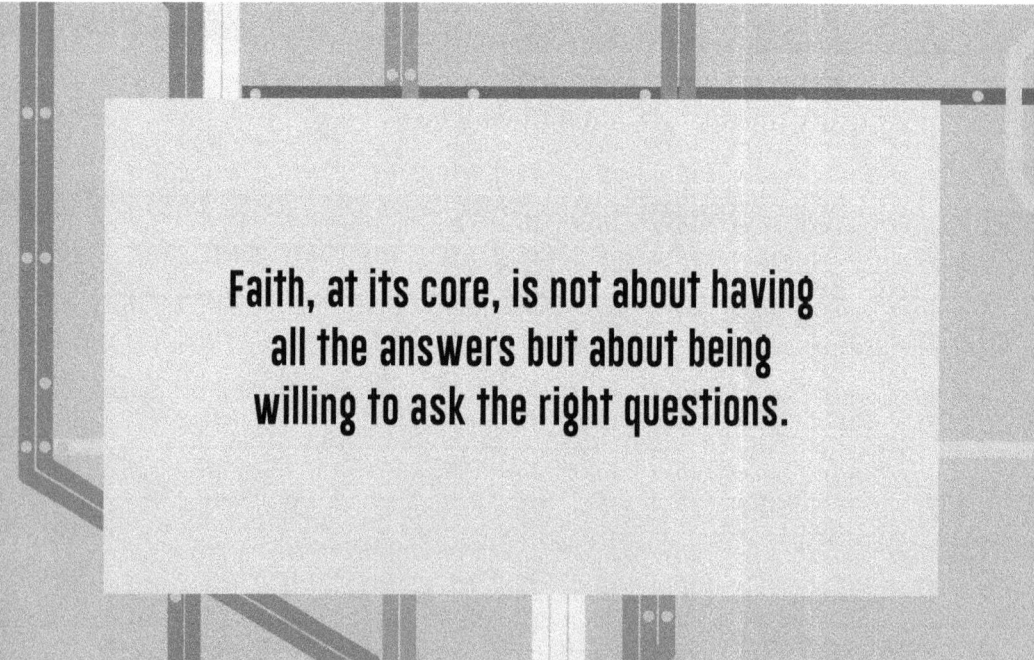

Faith, at its core, is not about having all the answers but about being willing to ask the right questions.

READING TIME

As you read Chapter 6: "On Deconstruction" in *Rethinking GOD with Tacos*, reflect on, and respond to the text by answering the following questions.

REFLECT AND TAKE ACTION:

What emotions emerge when you hear the term "deconstruction"? Do you tend to resist it or receive it—and what's driving that response?

_____
_____
_____
_____
_____
_____
_____
_____
_____
_____

Some people describe their spiritual path as one of deconstruction, but for others, it feels more like rebuilding from the ground up—reconstruction. How do those two words land differently for you?

_____
_____
_____
_____
_____
_____
_____
_____

> *"It is the glory of God to conceal a matter and the glory of kings to search it out."*
>
> **—Proverbs 25:2 (BSB)**

Consider the scripture above and answer the following questions:

What do you think this scripture has to do with deconstruction? How does it depart from or align with what you have been taught about deconstruction?

_____
_____
_____
_____
_____
_____
_____
_____

In what ways have you been discouraged from asking questions in your faith journey, and how might this scripture affirm your right—and responsibility—to search them out?

_____
_____
_____
_____
_____
_____
_____
_____

What structures in your understanding of God, church, or self have begun to crumble? What prompted their collapse? What do they look like rebuilt?

_____
_____
_____
_____

Have you ever been told that asking hard questions is a sign of rebellion or weak faith? How does this chapter challenge that belief?

_____
_____
_____
_____

Think about a belief you've deconstructed. What did you lose in letting it go—and what did you gain?

_____
_____
_____
_____
_____
_____
_____
_____

How do you distinguish between healthy deconstruction and destruction that leads to disconnection or despair?

_____
_____
_____
_____
_____
_____
_____
_____
_____

What area of your faith are you most afraid to question? Why? What might it look like to bring even that to Jesus?

_____
_____
_____
_____
_____
_____
_____
_____

If faith isn't about having all the answers, what new way of "being faithful" is this chapter inviting you to embrace?

_____
_____
_____
_____
_____
_____
_____
_____
_____

CHAPTER 7

TRINITARIAN FAITH
Guac, Queso, Salsa

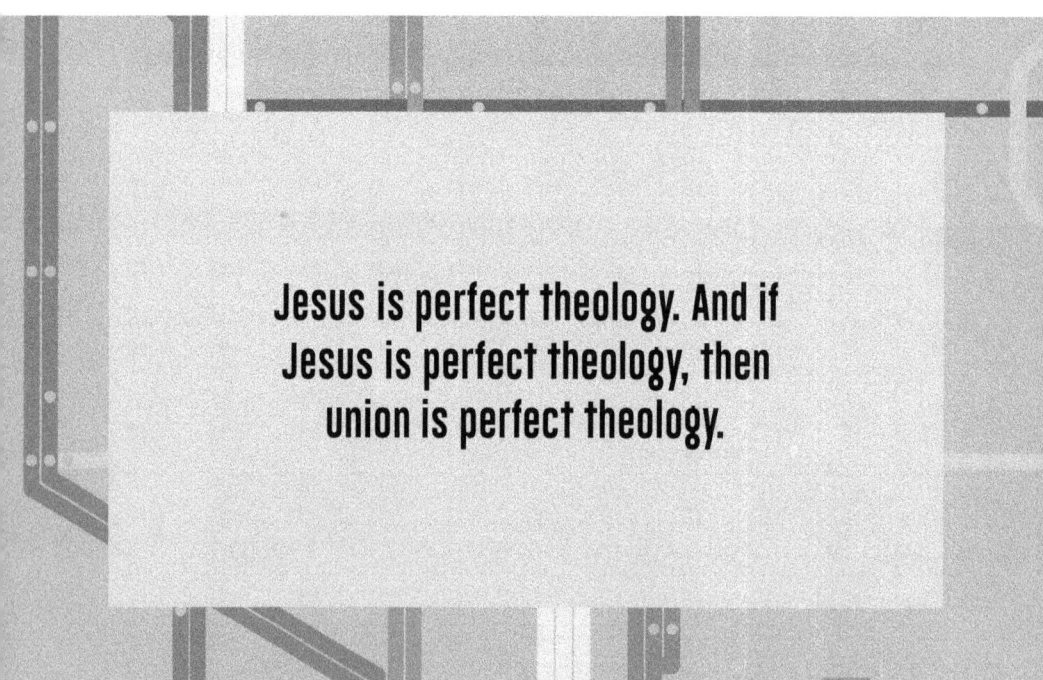

Jesus is perfect theology. And if Jesus is perfect theology, then union is perfect theology.

READING TIME

As you read Chapter 7: "Trinitarian Faith" in *Rethinking GOD with Tacos*, reflect on, and respond to the text by answering the following questions.

REFLECT AND TAKE ACTION:

What about the Trinity is meaningful to you, or what aspects of it challenge you?

_____
_____
_____
_____
_____
_____
_____
_____
_____
_____

What image comes to mind when you think of perichoresis—the divine circle dance? Where do you see yourself in that movement?

_____
_____
_____
_____
_____
_____
_____
_____
_____
_____

> *"Anyone who has seen me has seen the Father."*
>
> —John 14:9 (NIV)

Consider the scripture above and answer the following questions:

If seeing Jesus is seeing the Father, how does that confront any lingering beliefs that the Father is less kind, less compassionate, or more wrathful than Jesus?

_____
_____
_____
_____
_____
_____
_____
_____

What does this verse say about the unity and equality within the Trinity? What was your theology of trinitarian hierarchy before reading this chapter? How does it challenge any views you might have that place the Father above Jesus or treat the Spirit as lesser?

_____
_____
_____
_____
_____
_____
_____
_____

Jesus didn't come to create union but to awaken us to the union that already exists. What does that statement mean to you personally?

_____
_____
_____
_____

How does knowing that God has never been alone—and never lacked love—reshape your view of why you were created?

_____
_____
_____
_____
_____

What fears or beliefs might be holding you back from participating freely in the "eternal dance" of the Trinity?

_____
_____
_____
_____
_____
_____
_____
_____

Sometimes, a loss can lead to a crisis of faith—and an awakening to the relational love of God. Have you ever had a moment of deep loss that altered your theology? What did you discover?

_____
_____
_____
_____
_____
_____
_____
_____

The Trinity invites us into a relationship marked by mutuality, not performance. Where in your life are you still striving instead of resting in divine communion?

_____
_____
_____
_____
_____
_____
_____
_____

In what ways do you feel like your theology has been more influenced by Western individualism or hierarchy than by relational union, and what about this chapter challenges that?

_____
_____
_____
_____
_____
_____
_____
_____

CHAPTER 8

THE INCARNATION
When the Word Ate Tacos

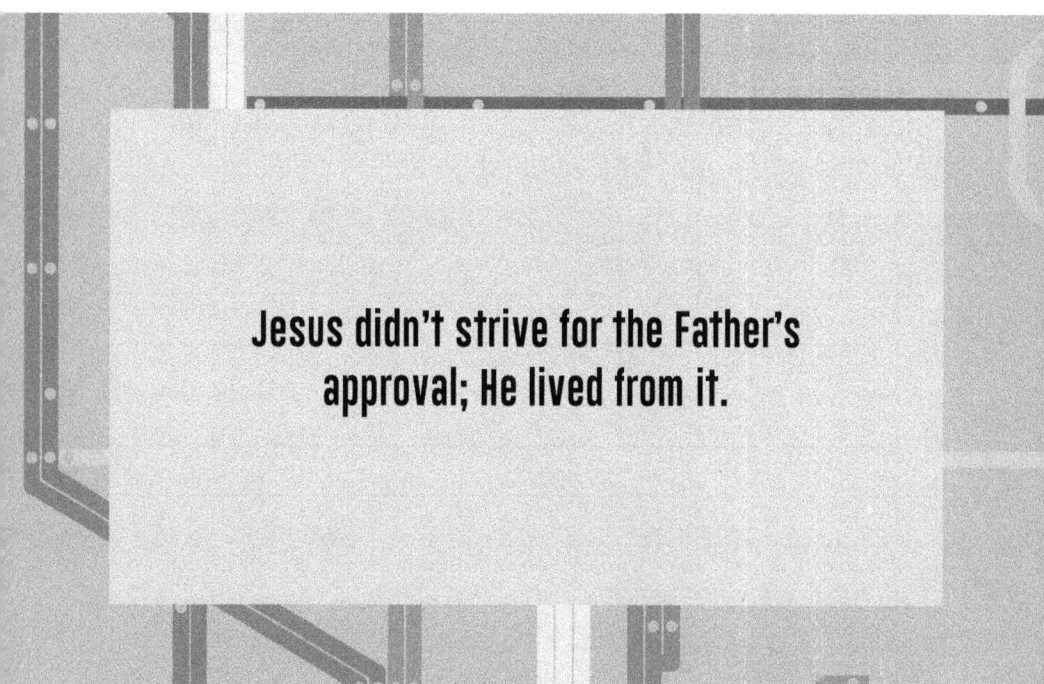

Jesus didn't strive for the Father's approval; He lived from it.

READING TIME

As you read Chapter 8: "The Incarnation" in *Rethinking GOD with Tacos*, reflect on, and respond to the text by answering the following questions.

REFLECT AND TAKE ACTION:

John Crowder calls Jesus "the union of creation to its Creator." If that's true, what does it reveal about the way you've compartmentalized the sacred and the secular in your life—and what needs to be reintegrated?

_____
_____
_____
_____
_____
_____
_____
_____

If union with God isn't something to earn but something to uncover, what false narratives or religious habits have kept you blind to it?

_____
_____
_____
_____
_____
_____
_____
_____

In what specific moments have you treated your humanity as a flaw rather than a dwelling place for God? What did that belief cost you?

_____
_____
_____
_____
_____
_____
_____

"The essence of your life adds value to God." What part of your life have you secretly believed was meaningless or unseen—and what would change if you believed it was sacred?

_____
_____
_____
_____
_____
_____
_____

Cherith Fee Nordling says Jesus didn't "put on humanity like a Halloween costume." If Jesus never planned to distance Himself from our nature, what does that say about the parts of yourself you still try to hide from God?

_____
_____
_____

"Your humanity was never the problem." Think of one belief, sermon, or system that convinced you otherwise. What would it look like to uproot it?

What specific past experience of suffering made you question whether God was truly with you? How would you reconstruct that memory through the lens of incarnation?

_____
_____
_____
_____
_____
_____
_____
_____
_____

Where are you still operating with an us-versus-them mindset—in politics, theology, or relationships? What would it cost you—and what would you gain—to live as if there is no "them"—only "us"?

_____
_____
_____
_____
_____
_____
_____

Where has fear trained you to anticipate failure or rejection more than beauty or breakthrough? What would change if your imagination belonged to love instead?

CHAPTER 9

IDENTITY
You Are What You Eat

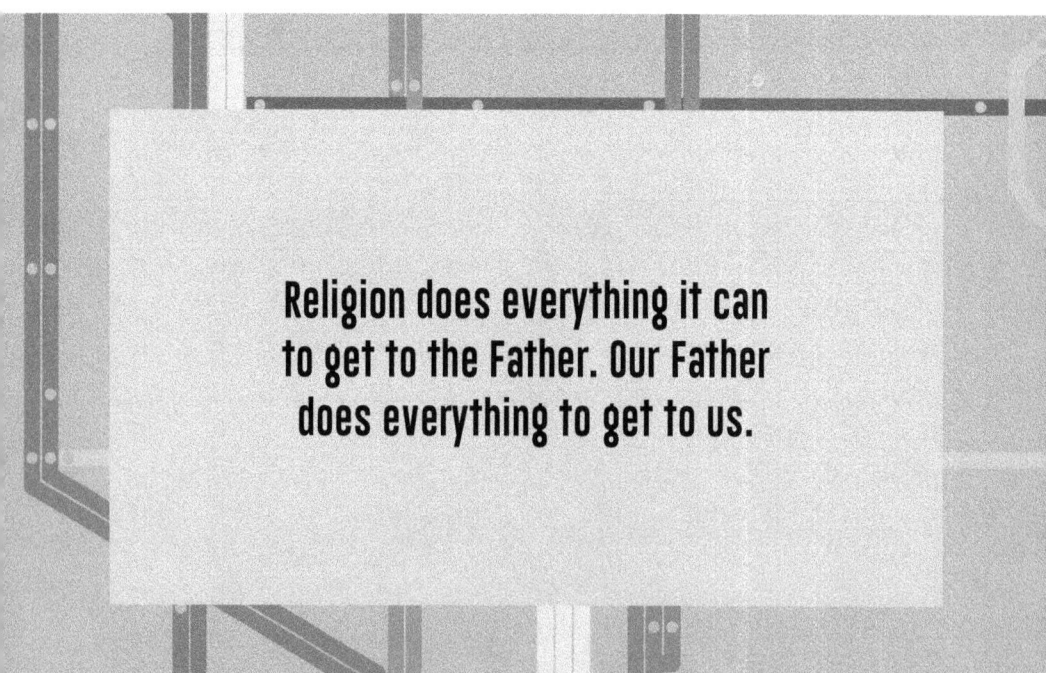

> Religion does everything it can to get to the Father. Our Father does everything to get to us.

READING TIME

As you read Chapter 9: "Identity" in *Rethinking GOD with Tacos*, reflect on, and respond to the text by answering the following questions.

REFLECT AND TAKE ACTION:

What moment or phrase in this chapter made you stop and think, Could that really be true about me?

_____
_____
_____
_____
_____

Which line or statement from Lloyd Clark's journey stood out to you the most, and why?

_____
_____
_____
_____
_____
_____
_____

Identity can only be discovered in relationship. What relationships have either hindered or helped your understanding of your true identity?

_____
_____
_____
_____
_____
_____

> *"This is the divine exchange: He who knew no sin embraced our distortion; he appeared to be without form; this was the mystery of God's prophetic poetry. He was disguised in our distorted image and marred with our iniquities; he took our sorrows, our pain and our shame to his grave and birthed his righteousness in us. He took our sins and we became his innocence."*
>
> **—2 Corinthians 5:21 (Mirror Translation)**

Consider the scripture above and answer the following questions:

If Jesus didn't just take your sin but became your shame, your sorrow, and your pain—what part of your identity have you unknowingly built around those wounds instead of His innocence?

_____

_____

_____

_____

_____

_____

When you read that "you became His innocence," what specific behaviors, thought patterns, or labels feel incompatible with that truth—and are you willing to confront them? Why or why not?

_____

_____

_____

_____

_____

_____

What accusations are shaping the way you see yourself? If God were to write you a letter directly confronting that lie, what truth would He speak over you instead?

_____
_____
_____
_____

What does it mean to live from love instead of striving for it? What would shift if you believed you were already fully loved?

_____
_____
_____
_____

Think of a time when someone saw the real you and didn't flinch. What can you glean from that as it relates to the way God sees you?

_____
_____
_____
_____
_____
_____
_____
_____

What parts of your "false self" are you still clinging to? What keeps you from letting them go?

_____
_____
_____
_____
_____
_____
_____
_____

How would your choices, habits, and relationships change if you believed your worth was never up for debate? Share an example in detail.

_____
_____
_____
_____
_____
_____
_____
_____

What messages from the Church (or from family, school, or society) taught you that you were outside the house or needed to earn your place at the table? Are those messages still influencing your faith?

_____
_____
_____
_____
_____
_____
_____
_____

CHAPTER 10

A PATH TO WHOLENESS
The Whole Enchilada

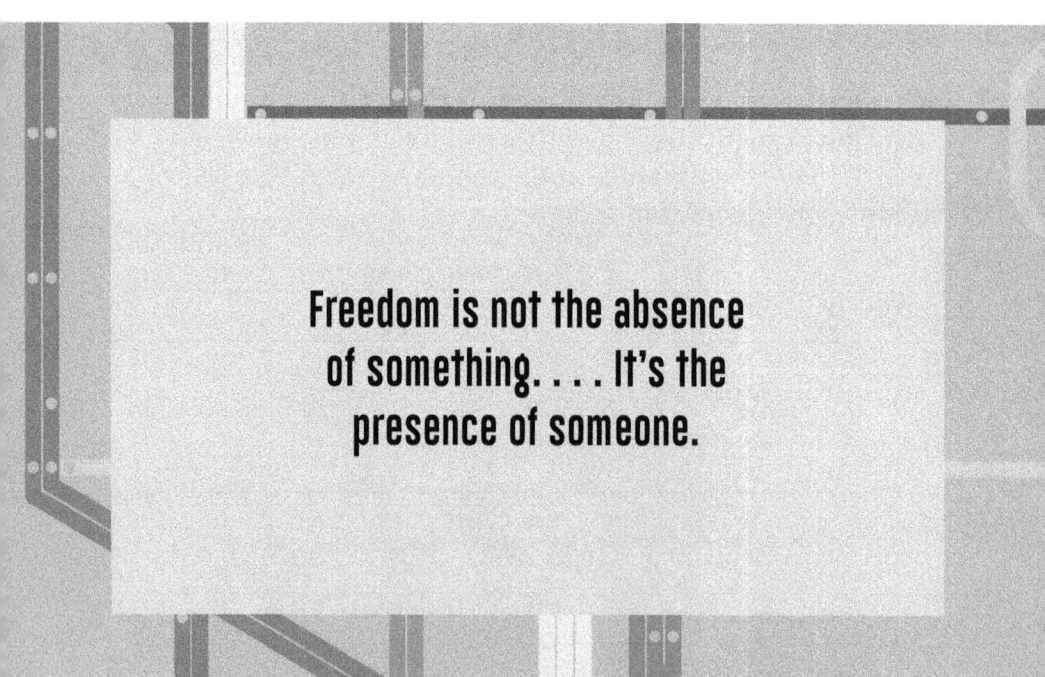

> Freedom is not the absence of something. . . . It's the presence of someone.

READING TIME

As you read Chapter 10: "A Path to Wholeness" in *Rethinking GOD with Tacos*, reflect on, and respond to the text by answering the following questions.

REFLECT AND TAKE ACTION:

Our brains don't have structures for fear, anxiety, or depression. Which of these learned responses has taken root in your life, and where might you have learned them?

_____
_____
_____
_____
_____
_____
_____
_____

When have you tried to "renew your mind" by forcing positivity or quoting scripture rather than inviting Gods loving thoughts about you to expose lies and rewrite your story? What has that avoidance cost you?

_____
_____
_____
_____
_____
_____
_____

What lie about yourself or your worth still feels more real than your belovedness?

What part of your personality have you treated like a permanent identity rather than a conditioned survival response?

Think about a trait you've suppressed or minimized because it didn't feel "safe" to express. How might reintegrating that part of you contribute to your wholeness today?

___

What's one area of your life where you've equated progress with "being less broken" rather than becoming more whole? Write down what it would look like to shift that narrative.

___

Repentance means to rethink who God is in light of Jesus and rediscover who you are through His love. This approach to repentance can impact your entire reality. What's one belief you've inherited that you now realize needs to be rethought from the ground up?

___

What paradigm shift did this chapter introduce that challenged your previous assumptions about what it means to be whole?

CHAPTER 11

THE CHURCH
We're in This Taco-gether

Christian worship is a dinner party.

READING TIME

As you read Chapter 11: "The Church" in Rethinking GOD with Tacos, reflect on, and respond to the text by answering the following questions.

REFLECT AND TAKE ACTION:

How do you discern between God's new work and your own discomfort with change?

_____
_____
_____
_____
_____
_____
_____
_____

What part of your church experience has contributed to the idea that leadership equals certainty and control? How has that shaped your perception of spiritual authority?

_____
_____
_____
_____
_____
_____
_____
_____

> "Behold, I am doing a new thing; now it springs forth, do you not perceive it? I will make a way in the wilderness and rivers in the desert."
>
> —Isaiah 43:19 (ESV)

Consider the scripture above and answer the following questions:

How can you tell when a church claims to preach reconciliation but fails to practice it in its relationships, leadership, or community life?

_____
_____
_____
_____
_____
_____
_____

What old structures, traditions, or church models have become your "wilderness"—dry places you return to out of comfort rather than calling?

_____
_____
_____
_____
_____
_____
_____
_____

When have you perceived God doing a new thing in your understanding of church but resisted it out of loyalty to the familiar?

_____
_____
_____
_____
_____
_____
_____
_____
_____
_____

David Hewitt offers a vision of participatory, relational church. How does your current spiritual community reflect (or resist) that vision? Where do you feel called to contribute but haven't been invited or empowered to do so?

_____
_____
_____
_____
_____
_____
_____

When have you mistaken institutional loyalty for spiritual maturity? How can you distinguish the two going forward?

_____
_____
_____
_____
_____
_____
_____

In what ways have you treated the Church more as a product to consume than a family to serve and build? What needs to change in your weekly rhythms or mindset to align with God's vision for ecclesia?

_____
_____
_____
_____
_____
_____
_____
_____

What did this chapter affirm about the beauty and power of the Church that you had forgotten? How did it stir your hope again?

_____
_____
_____
_____
_____
_____
_____
_____

CHAPTER 12

THE KINGDOM
Righteousness, Peace, and Pico de Gallo

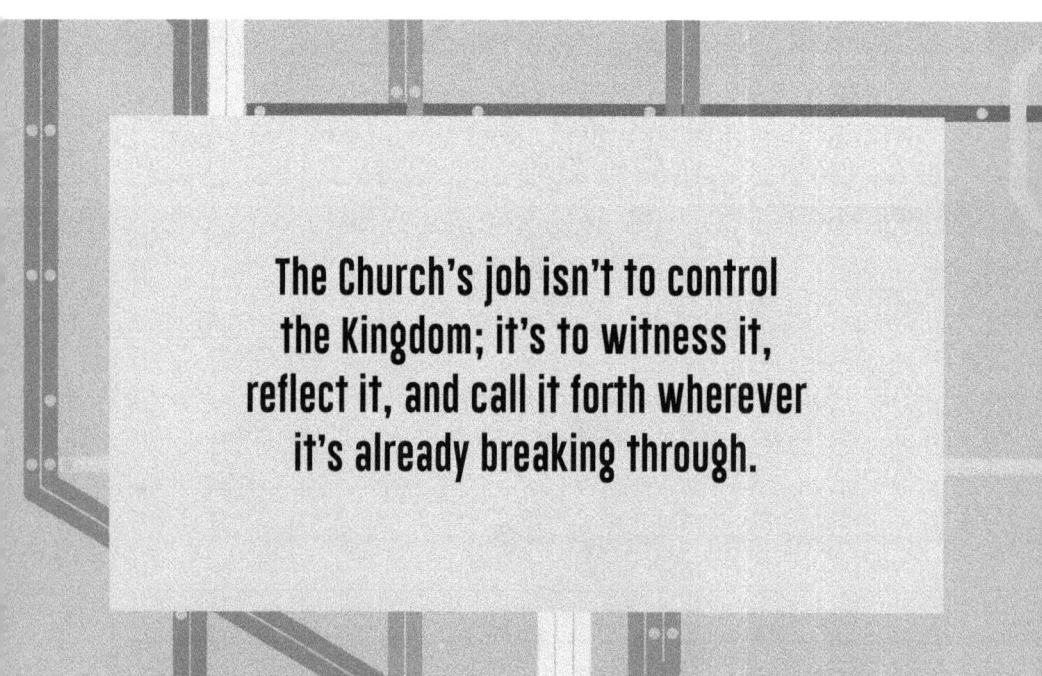

> The Church's job isn't to control the Kingdom; it's to witness it, reflect it, and call it forth wherever it's already breaking through.

READING TIME

As you read Chapter 12: "The Kingdom" in *Rethinking GOD with Tacos*, reflect on, and respond to the text by answering the following questions.

REFLECT AND TAKE ACTION:

When you picture the Kingdom of God, what images come to mind—and where did those images originate? How have they shaped the way you relate to God?

_____
_____
_____
_____
_____
_____
_____
_____

Which aspect of the Kingdom presented in this chapter (family, union, healing, rest, governance, etc.) challenged your current understanding the most, and why?

_____
_____
_____
_____
_____
_____
_____
_____

> *"Being asked by the Pharisees when the kingdom of God would come, he answered them, 'The kingdom of God is not coming in ways that can be observed, nor will they say, "Look, here it is!" or "There!" for behold, the kingdom of God is in the midst of you.'"*
>
> —Luke 17:20-21 (ESV)

Consider the scripture above and answer the following questions:

Jesus says the Kingdom is not something observable—but within. In what ways have you been conditioned to look outward or ahead rather than inward and present? What would change if you believed the Kingdom was truly within you right now?

_____
_____
_____
_____
_____
_____

If the Kingdom isn't a far-off destination but an inner reality, what lies of separation are you still holding onto that keep you from experiencing it?

_____
_____
_____
_____
_____
_____

Think of a time when striving, hierarchy, or performance was promoted as a pathway to intimacy with God. How did that affect your faith journey?

_____
_____
_____
_____

Chris Gore said, "Desperation is not the prerequisite for your miracle." How does that statement confront your current theology or emotional posture before God?

_____
_____
_____
_____

If spiritual maturity is discovering what's already true instead of achieving something new, what old metric of "growth" do you need to let go of?

_____
_____
_____
_____
_____
_____
_____

"Religion is mankind's desperate attempt to meet God, whereas the Kingdom is God meeting humanity in its brokenness." How have you experienced this contrast in your life—and which narrative are you living from now?

_____
_____
_____
_____
_____
_____
_____
_____

Make two short lists:

List three beliefs you've held about the Kingdom that were shaped more by religion than by Jesus.

1._____
2._____
3._____

List three new truths this chapter has helped you see about the Kingdom's nature, timing, or accessibility.

1._____
2._____
3._____

What stands out when you compare the two?

_____
_____
_____
_____
_____
_____
_____
_____

CHAPTER 13

GRACE
Bottomless Margaritas

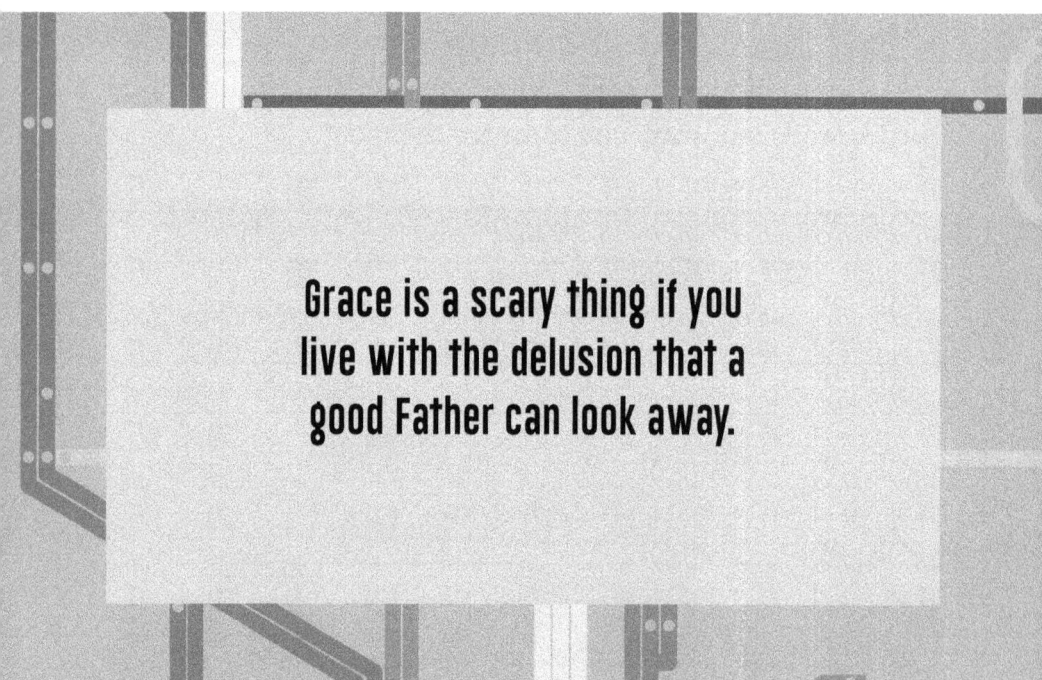

Grace is a scary thing if you live with the delusion that a good Father can look away.

READING TIME

As you read Chapter 13: "Grace" in *Rethinking GOD with Tacos*, reflect on, and respond to the text by answering the following questions.

REFLECT AND TAKE ACTION:

In your own words, what does it mean to "balance" grace? In what ways does this concept resonate with you?

_____
_____
_____
_____
_____
_____
_____
_____
_____

Have you ever instinctively tried to "balance" grace? What underlying belief about God or people were you trying to protect?

_____
_____
_____
_____
_____
_____
_____
_____

> *"What shall we say, then? Shall we go on sinning so that grace may increase? By no means! We are those who have died to sin; how can we live in it any longer?"*
>
> **—Romans 6:1-2 (NIV)**

Consider the scripture above and answer the following questions:

Paul anticipates the backlash to radical grace by addressing the concern that it will promote sin. What does your gut reaction to this verse reveal about how you perceive grace—dangerous and permissive or transformative and empowering?

_____

_____

_____

_____

_____

_____

_____

Reflect on the phrase, "We are those who have died to sin." In what specific ways have you continued to relate to sin as if it still holds power over you? What might shift if you truly believed you were dead to it?

_____

_____

_____

_____

_____

_____

_____

What emotions surface when you hear someone say, "You can't abuse grace"? To what extent do you believe that, and what personal or church experiences have made that statement feel threatening—or liberating?

_____
_____
_____
_____
_____

Reflect on a moment in your life when grace felt "too good to be true." What would change if you embraced it as "too good not to be true"?

_____
_____
_____
_____
_____

"Behavior follows identity." In what ways have you tried to behave your way into identity rather than allowing identity to transform your behavior?

_____
_____
_____
_____
_____
_____
_____
_____

What's one lingering belief you still wrestle with about God's posture toward you when you mess up? How does this chapter invite you to confront and replace that belief?

_____
_____
_____
_____
_____
_____
_____
_____

Why do you think some people feel both relieved and uneasy when they hear that grace means they don't have to earn God's love?

_____
_____
_____
_____
_____
_____
_____
_____

If someone asked you to define God's grace today, how would your response differ from how you would have explained it before reading this chapter?

_____
_____
_____
_____
_____
_____
_____
_____

CHAPTER 14

INCLUSION
You Belong, Queso Closed

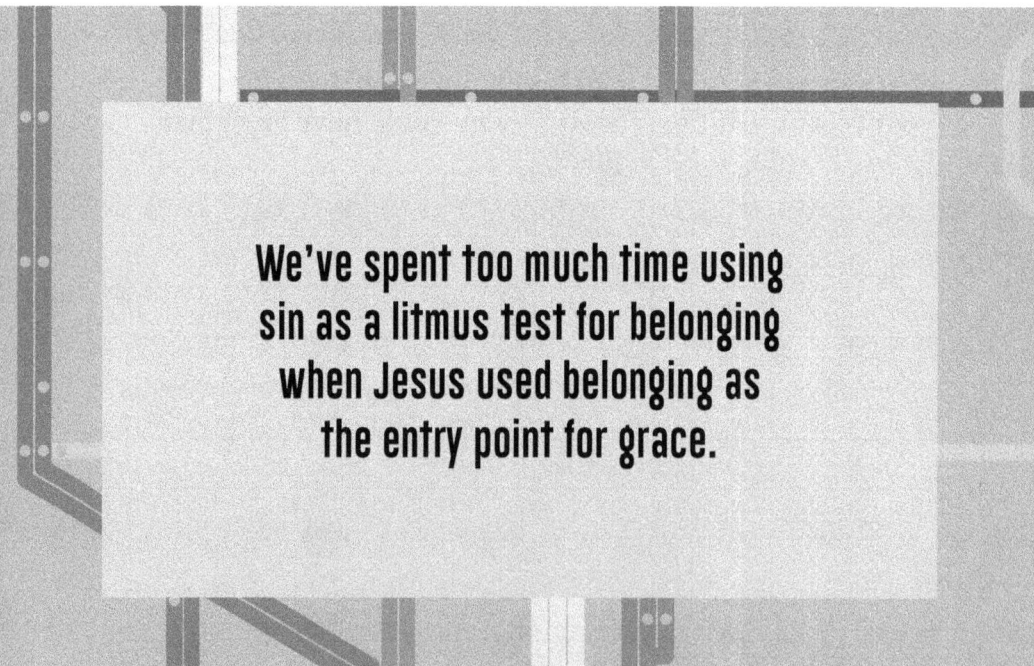

> We've spent too much time using sin as a litmus test for belonging when Jesus used belonging as the entry point for grace.

READING TIME

As you read Chapter 14: "Inclusion" in *Rethinking GOD with Tacos*, reflect on, and respond to the text by answering the following questions.

REFLECT AND TAKE ACTION:

In what subtle ways have you categorized people as "insiders" or "outsiders" in your own mind or church culture?

_____
_____
_____
_____
_____
_____
_____
_____
_____
_____

Can you recall a moment when someone's dignity was restored because of inclusion? What role did love—not doctrine—play in that transformation?

_____
_____
_____
_____
_____
_____
_____
_____
_____
_____

> *"Truly I understand that God shows no partiality."*
> —**Acts 10:34 (ESV)**

Consider the scripture above and answer the following questions:

When Peter said, "God shows no partiality," what did that overturn in his belief system? What might it overturn in yours?

_____

_____

_____

_____

_____

_____

_____

If God doesn't play favorites, where in your theology or church tradition might favoritism still be present?

_____

_____

_____

_____

_____

_____

_____

What parts of your faith community still operate from a "us vs. them" mindset, even if unintentionally?

_____

_____

Who would it challenge you most to sit next to at church—and what does that reveal? Is it consistent with Jesus's life and message?

If your church leadership were to shift toward radical inclusion, what resistance might they face—and from where?

_____
_____
_____
_____
_____
_____
_____
_____

Mark Appleyard said, "Dignity is protecting the image of God in someone." Where have you failed to do this? Where can you start today?

_____
_____
_____
_____
_____
_____
_____
_____
_____

Describe a time when you witnessed someone being excluded in the Church. What did you do in that moment, and what do you wish you had done differently?

_____
_____
_____
_____
_____
_____
_____
_____

How has your understanding of inclusion shifted after reading this chapter?

_____
_____
_____
_____
_____
_____
_____
_____
_____

CHAPTER 15

RETHINKING UNIVERSALISM
Unlimited Chips and Salsa

> If we can imagine God doing less, then we've misunderstood the heart of the Father.

READING TIME

As you read Chapter 15: "Rethinking Universalism" in *Rethinking GOD with Tacos*, reflect on, and respond to the text by answering the following questions.

REFLECT AND TAKE ACTION:

When you reflect on the idea that all were included in Christ's death and resurrection, what questions or resistance does that stir in you?

_____
_____
_____
_____
_____
_____
_____
_____
_____

What's a truth about God's love you've been hesitant to share for fear of rejection?

_____
_____
_____
_____
_____
_____
_____
_____
_____

> *"We love because He first loved."*
>
> **—1 John 4:19 (ESV)**

Consider the scripture above and answer the following questions:

How does knowing that God's love initiated your ability to love reshape the way you view people who reject Him, resist church, or live outside your moral framework?

_____
_____
_____
_____
_____
_____

If God's love is what enables you to love, what parts of yourself have you withheld from loving because you believed He hadn't fully accepted them either?

_____
_____
_____
_____
_____
_____

In what ways has your understanding of God's love expanded as you've explored the idea that His love is the starting point, not the reward?

_____
_____

_____
_____
_____
_____
_____

Where do you still wrestle with the idea that God's judgment is restorative and not punitive? What would it take for you to release the latter?

_____
_____
_____
_____
_____
_____
_____

When have you feared that God's love or presence might be withdrawn based on something you did or didn't do? How does seeing grace as a covenant challenge that fear?

_____
_____
_____
_____
_____
_____
_____
_____

Consider this statement: "If hell exists eternally, then evil has the last word, not grace." What emotions rise in you as you consider that? What's at stake for you in which grace gets the final word?

_____
_____
_____
_____
_____
_____
_____
_____

What does it mean to you to "rediscover" rather than invent universalistic reconciliation?

_____
_____
_____
_____
_____
_____
_____
_____

List three new ideas that challenged you the most in this chapter:

1._____
_____
_____

2._____
_____
_____

3._____
_____
_____

CHAPTER 16

RETHINKING HELL
Nacho Eternal Punishment

> Hell is the distortion of the human condition, not God separating Himself from us.

READING TIME

As you read Chapter 16: "Rethinking Hell" in *Rethinking GOD with Tacos*, reflect on, and respond to the text by answering the following questions.

REFLECT AND TAKE ACTION:

How have you historically understood eternal punishment, and what emotions surface when you consider the possibility that it may not be what you were taught? Why do you think that is?

_____
_____
_____
_____
_____
_____
_____
_____
_____

According to the chapter, how has a fear of hell been used as a tool in the Western Church, and how has that personally shaped your spiritual formation?

_____
_____
_____
_____
_____
_____
_____
_____
_____
_____

> *"For as in Adam all die, so in Christ all will be made alive."*
>
> **— 1 Corinthians 15:22 (NIV)**

Consider the scripture above and answer the following questions:

Paul places all of humanity both in Adam and in Christ in this verse. How does this challenge traditional notions of exclusion or eternal punishment for some?

_____
_____
_____
_____
_____
_____

Reflect on your inherited theological view of hell. In what ways does this verse invite you to reexamine or reframe it?

_____
_____
_____
_____
_____
_____
_____

In what ways has the doctrine of penal substitution shaped your view of God's love? After reading this chapter, what questions or tensions do you now feel?

_____

In your own words, how could hell actually be a restorative process? How does it fit into relational theology?

What fear rises up in you when you imagine a God who refuses to punish eternally—even the "worst" among us?

_____
_____
_____
_____
_____
_____
_____

Have you ever shared (or feared sharing) a view of hell that differs from your church or community's doctrine? What was the cost—or what do you fear it would be—and how does that cost reveal the weight of tradition over transformation?

_____
_____
_____
_____
_____
_____
_____

The chapter repeatedly emphasizes union as the "third option." Think of a time when you felt forced to choose between two extremes in faith. How might union have offered a better way?

_____
_____
_____
_____
_____
_____
_____
_____

What story—personal or biblical—would you have to revisit and reinterpret to see a God who restores rather than punishes forever?

_____
_____
_____
_____
_____
_____
_____
_____

CHAPTER 17

JUSTICE
A Taco for a Taco

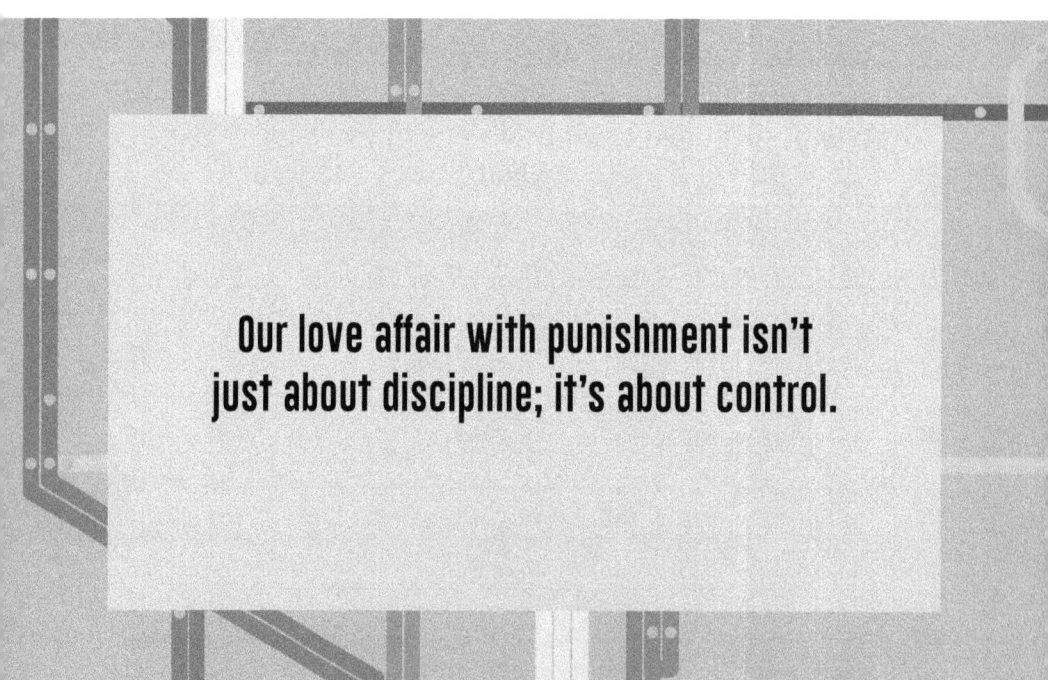

Our love affair with punishment isn't just about discipline; it's about control.

READING TIME

As you read Chapter 17: "Justice" in *Rethinking GOD with Tacos*, reflect on, and respond to the text by answering the following questions.

REFLECT AND TAKE ACTION:

Have you ever used fear, shame, or withdrawal to influence someone's behavior? Reflect on what that reveals about your image of God— and how it might be time to revise that view.

_____
_____
_____
_____
_____
_____
_____
_____
_____

Describe a time when you saw "justice" carried out, but it didn't feel just. How would restorative justice have looked different in that scenario?

_____
_____
_____
_____
_____
_____
_____
_____
_____

> "But I say, love your enemies! Pray for those who persecute you!"
>
> **—Matthew 5:44 (NLT)**

Consider the scripture above and answer the following questions:

Jesus commands us to love our enemies. What does that demand of you—not in theory but in a current or past situation where you've been deeply wronged?

_____
_____
_____
_____
_____
_____
_____
_____

God's justice is restorative rather than retaliatory; how might you apply Matthew 5:44 to the systems or people you tend to want punished?

_____
_____
_____
_____
_____
_____
_____
_____

List 2–3 beliefs you grew up with about God's justice or punishment. Then next to each one, write what you think the restorative alternative might be—and how believing it would change how you live, lead, or love.

1. _____
_____
_____
_____

2. _____
_____
_____
_____

3. _____
_____
_____
_____

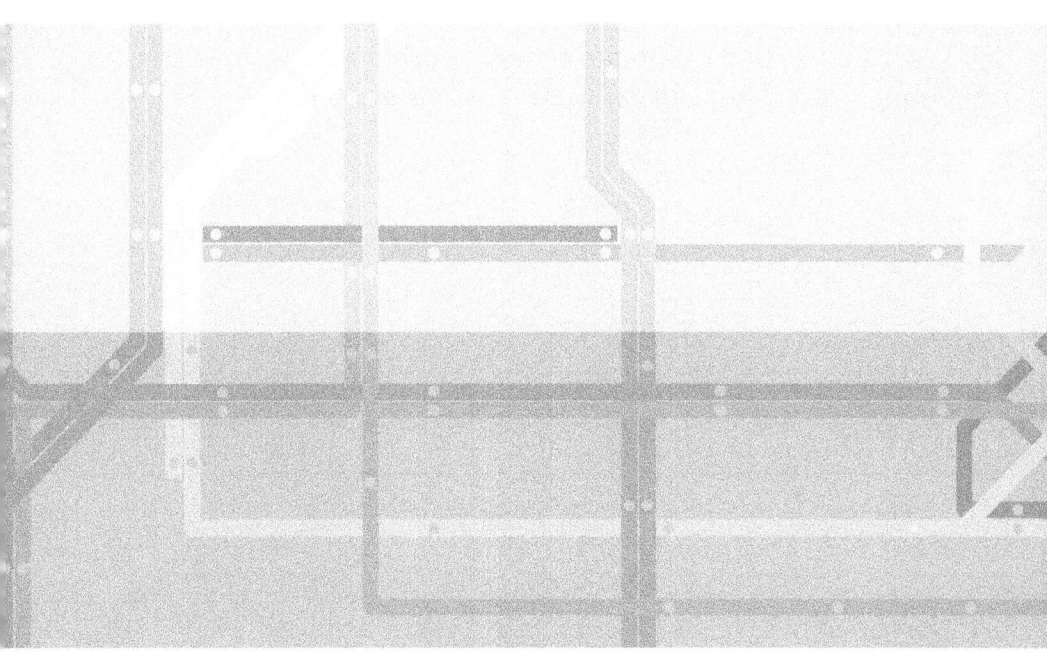

What does the phrase "God's wrath is against what's killing us, not against us" reveal about your inherited view of God?

_____
_____
_____
_____
_____
_____
_____

How does the cross—humanity's greatest act of violence turned into God's ultimate act of restorative love—upend your belief that justice must end in punishment?

_____
_____
_____
_____
_____
_____
_____
_____

In what ways does this chapter expose the gap between what you believe about God and how you practice faith toward those you consider enemies?

_____
_____
_____
_____
_____
_____
_____
_____

Which parts of this chapter made you feel most defensive? Why do you think that is? Were there any parts that made you feel unexpectedly relieved or hopeful? What do those contrasting reactions reveal about how you view justice, love, and God?

_____
_____
_____
_____
_____
_____
_____
_____

CHAPTER 18

THE LONG ARC OF LOVE
Slow-Cooked, Like Carnitas

Jesus didn't die for us—He died as us.

READING TIME

As you read Chapter 18: "The Long Arc of Love" in *Rethinking GOD with Tacos*, reflect on, and respond to the text by answering the following questions.

REFLECT AND TAKE ACTION:

Where are you right now in your spiritual journey—mentally, emotionally, or theologically—and how does it affect you to realize that God isn't concerned with where you are, only that He's inviting you into more?

_____
_____
_____
_____
_____
_____
_____
_____
_____

Think of a theological position or church tradition you grew up with. When you hold it up to the life and teachings of Jesus, where does it fall short?

_____
_____
_____
_____
_____
_____
_____
_____
_____

Malcolm Smith calls the parable of the prodigal son a "war cry." What religious constructs does that story demolish in your life?

___

What illusions of separation have you carried that still affect how you relate to God or others?

___

What does it mean for you to "tell the world what you see" through Christ's lens?

___

If "every person is on their Emmaus Road," how should that influence the way you view people with whom you deeply disagree?

How do you personally distinguish between control-based religion and the relational connection God offers?

_____
_____
_____
_____
_____
_____
_____
_____
_____
_____

"Jesus didn't die for us—He died as us." What theological systems or assumptions are challenged by this statement?

_____
_____
_____
_____
_____
_____
_____
_____
_____
_____

If "the long arc of love" is the beginning, middle, and end of the gospel story, how does that reshape the way you read Scripture, interact with others, and understand your purpose?

_____
_____
_____
_____
_____
_____
_____

Looking back over this entire journey, what is one belief, assumption, or habit that you now feel compelled to rethink or release—and what's the first courageous step you'll take to move forward in light of what you've discovered?

_____
_____
_____
_____
_____
_____
_____

www.ingramcontent.com/pod-product-compliance
Lightning Source LLC
Chambersburg PA
CBHW070049100426
42734CB00040B/2885